it starts with
⋯⟩✦ Y O U ✦⟨⋯

THIS JOURNAL BELONGS TO:

_____

YOU ARE THE MAGIC YOU SEEK

A JOURNAL FOR LOOKING WITHIN

By Kristen Drozdowski

CHRONICLE BOOKS

SAN FRANCISCO

ISBN: 978-1-4521-8480-7

MANUFACTURED IN CHINA.

10 9 8 7 6 5 4 3

CHRONICLE BOOKS AND GIFTS ARE AVAILABLE AT
SPECIAL QUANTITY DISCOUNTS TO CORPORATIONS,
PROFESSIONAL ASSOCIATIONS, LITERACY PROGRAMS,
AND OTHER ORGANIZATIONS. FOR DETAILS AND
DISCOUNT INFORMATION, PLEASE CONTACT OUR
PREMIUMS DEPARTMENT AT
CORPORATESALES @ CHRONICLEBOOKS.COM
OR AT 1-800-759-0190.

CHRONICLE BOOKS LLC
680 SECOND STREET
SAN FRANCISCO, CALIFORNIA 94107

WWW.CHRONICLEBOOKS.COM

BEGIN ANYWHERE

THIS JOURNAL WILL HELP YOU ACCESS YOUR INNER WISDOM. HERE YOU WILL FIND WORDS OF ENCOURAGEMENT, PRACTICES, AND PROMPTS THAT WILL PUT YOU IN TOUCH WITH DEEPER LAYERS OF YOURSELF. THE JOURNALING QUESTIONS WILL ENCOURAGE THE ANSWERS YOU ALREADY HAVE INSIDE YOU TO COME FORWARD.

YOU ARE WHERE THE REAL MAGIC BEGINS:

AS YOU RESPOND TO THE PROMPTS, YOU'LL PRACTICE BEING YOUR OWN GUIDE. MORE THOUGHTS CAN BE ADDED OVER TIME, AND YOU CAN LOOK BACK ON THEM FOR A DOSE OF *your own personal medicine.*

THE WAY YOU APPROACH THIS JOURNAL IS UP TO YOU. FEEL FREE TO DIP IN AND OUT, FLIP THROUGH UNTIL YOU FIND WHAT SPEAKS TO YOU IN THAT MOMENT, OR FOLLOW IT FROM START TO FINISH. GET CREATIVE AND ♡ *ENJOY YOURSELF!* ♡

YOU
KNOW IT
WHEN YOU
FEEL IT

WHAT ARE SIGNS THAT YOUR INTUITION IS SPEAKING TO YOU?

WAYS TO ACTIVATE YOUR INTUITIVE NATURE:

CARVE OUT MOMENTS OF SILENCE.

SPEND TIME OUTSIDE.

INTERACT WITH *natural elements.*

~ DISTANCE YOURSELF FROM ~ TECHNOLOGY & ARTIFICIAL LIGHT.

PAY CLOSE ATTENTION TO YOUR DREAMS.

TAKE NOTICE

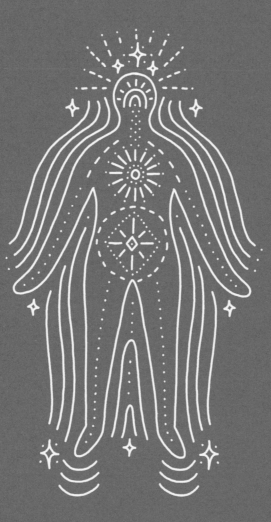

OF YOUR EMOTIONS
CREATING SIGNALS IN THE BODY
LIKE LITTLE MESSAGES.

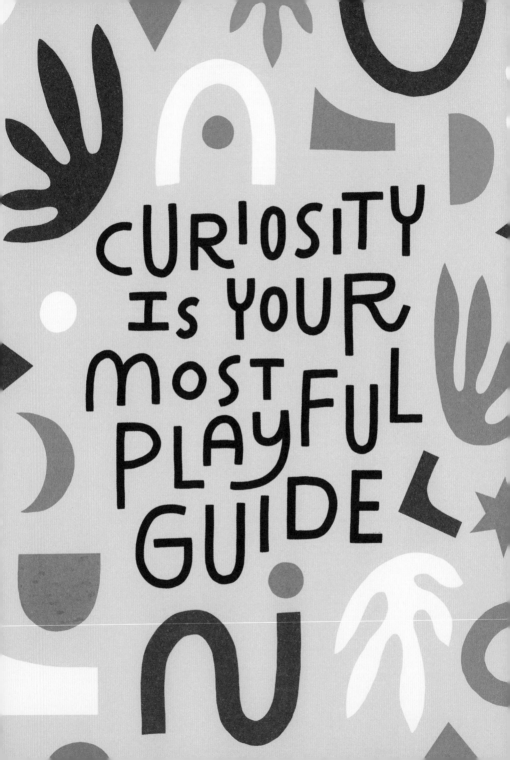

WHAT HAVE YOU ALWAYS WANTED TO DO OR LEARN MORE ABOUT?

GIVE YOURSELF PERMISSION TO FOLLOW CURIOSITY.

A STEP-BY-STEP ACTION PLAN

STEP 1:

THINK ABOUT SOMETHING THAT INTRIGUES YOU.

STEP 2:

REALIZE THAT THIS PERSISTENT CURIOSITY COULD BE A DOOR TO *SOMETHING AMAZING.*

MAYBE THERE IS HIDDEN MAGIC IN THERE,

WAITING PATIENTLY FOR YOU TO COME & FIND IT.

STEP 3: ON A BRIGHT AND CLEAR MORNING, DECIDE THAT

TODAY IS THE DAY

STEP 4: ACKNOWLEDGE ANY LITTLE VOICE TELLING YOU THERE IS "MORE IMPORTANT WORK TO DO." THANK IT FOR THE CONCERN BUT KINDLY ASSERT THAT LIFE IS SHORT AND THIS IS IMPORTANT WORK.

STEP 5: PROCEED WITH A SENSE OF WONDER & CHILDLIKE FREEDOM.

ALLOWING YOURSELF THIS TIME IS A GIFT.

GET
CARRIED
AWAY AND
SEE
WHAT
HAPPENS

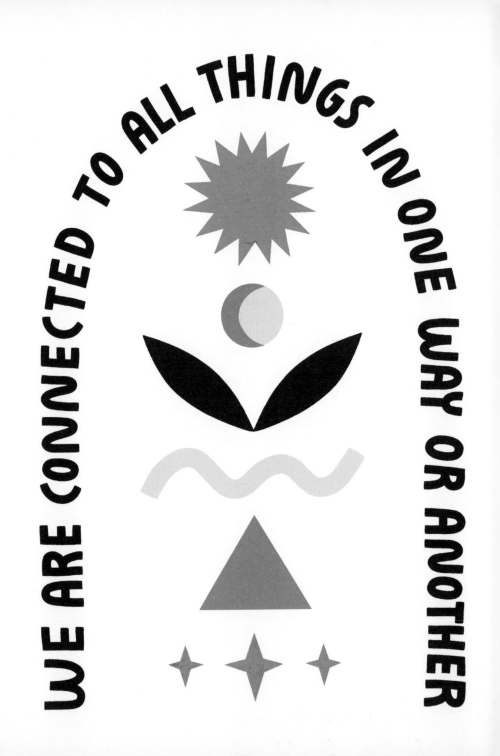

WE ARE CONNECTED TO ALL THINGS IN ONE WAY OR ANOTHER

WHAT CONNECTIONS SUPPORT YOU?

··· YOU ARE YOUR BEST GUIDE ····
BUT *YOU ARE NOT ALONE!*
THE POSITIVE RELATIONSHIPS WE HAVE WITH
PEOPLE, PLACES, AND OUR SURROUNDINGS
CAN HELP BRING OUT THE BEST IN US.

wholesome things
TO connect with:

CLOSE

FRIENDS

NATIVE
PLANTS

FAVORITE
ANIMALS

A BODY

OF WATER

THE EARTH

COMMUNITY

THE SUN, THE MOON & THE LIMITLESS SKY

BOOKS, ART & MUSIC

♡ ♡ ♡ SOMEONE YOU LOVE ♡ ♡ ♡

YOUR HEART-BEAT

YOUR BREATH

YOUR INNER VOICE

THE IDEA THAT IT'S ALSO OK TO DISCONNECT FROM THINGS THAT DEPLETE YOU.

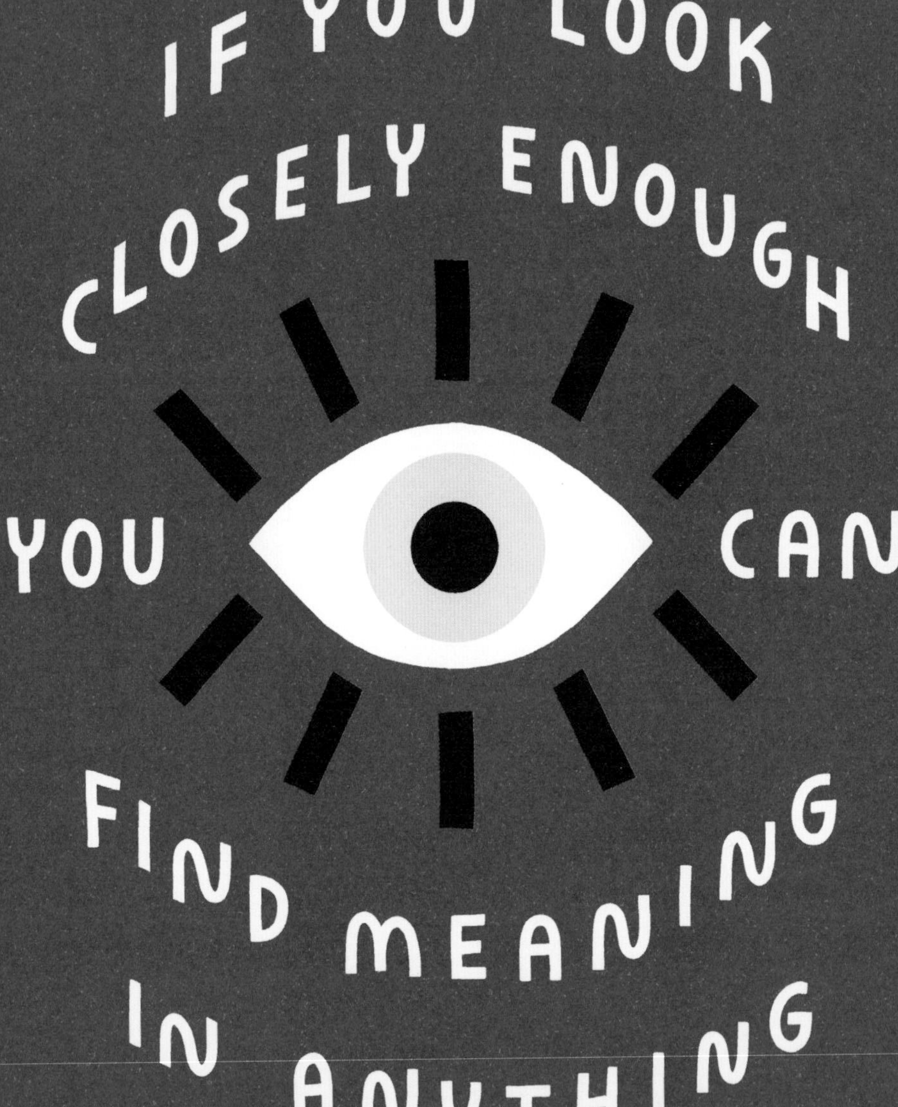
IF YOU LOOK
CLOSELY ENOUGH
YOU
CAN
FIND MEANING
IN ANYTHING

WHAT CAN YOU DO TO BE PRESENT IN YOUR SURROUNDINGS?

PRACTICE

☩ STILLNESS: ☩

STEP 1: FIND A GOOD TIME & PLACE TO TAKE A NICE DEEP BREATH.

STEP 2: NOTICE THE MOVEMENT OF YOUR THOUGHTS.

THE MIND IS COMPLEX, AND ITS DEFAULT MODE IS TO BE WILD AND FREE.

STEP 3: MAKE A CONSCIOUS EFFORT TO SHIFT YOUR AWARENESS AWAY FROM THOUGHT AND INTO YOUR ENVIRONMENT.

STEP 4: USING YOUR SENSES, PICK UP ON SOME SUBTLE THINGS HAPPENING AROUND YOU. MAYBE THERE ARE SMALL MOMENTS AND FASCINATING DETAILS JUST WAITING TO BE NOTICED.

STEP 5: CHOOSE ONE THING AROUND YOU THAT CALLS FOR YOUR ATTENTION.

EXAMPLES:

A CANDLE FLAME

THE DROP OF A FAUCET

QUIET STATIC NOISE

YOUR BREATH

THE WIND

A PLEASANT SHADOW

AN INTERESTING SHAPE

THE FEELING OF GRAVITY

ATTEND TO EVERY DETAIL.

LET EACH ONE CAPTIVATE YOU.

WHAT APPROACHES CAN YOU TAKE TO APPRECIATING YOUR BODY?

A PRACTICE FOR LOVING YOUR BODY

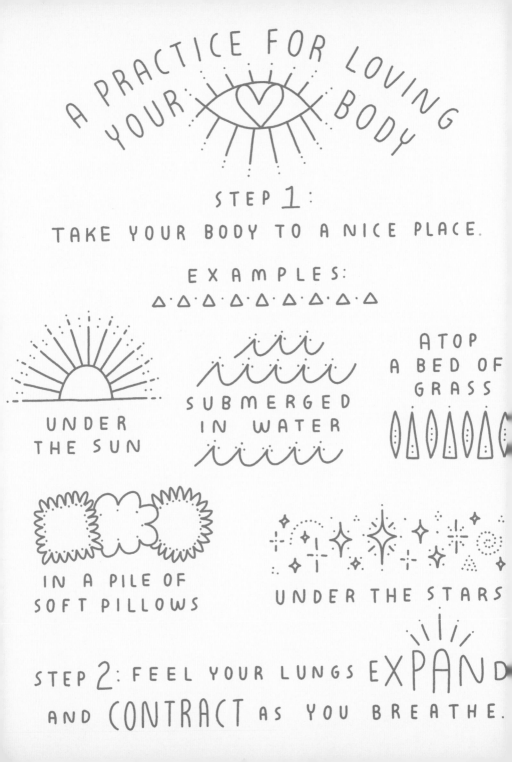

STEP 1:

TAKE YOUR BODY TO A NICE PLACE.

EXAMPLES:

UNDER THE SUN

SUBMERGED IN WATER

ATOP A BED OF GRASS

IN A PILE OF SOFT PILLOWS

UNDER THE STARS

STEP 2: FEEL YOUR LUNGS EXPAND AND CONTRACT AS YOU BREATHE.

STEP 3: ONCE YOU FEEL SETTLED, TAKE A MOMENT TO NOTICE EACH AND EVERY PART OF YOUR BODY, CELEBRATING IT *without judgment.*

STEP 4: GO A BIT FURTHER BY REALLY FEELING YOURSELF IN YOUR BODY.

MOVE AROUND A LITTLE! HOLD YOURSELF. MAKE YOURSELF AT HOME.

STEP 5: IF YOU START TO NOTICE ANY STORIES COME UP ABOUT HOW YOUR BODY SHOULD AND SHOULD NOT LOOK, IMAGINE THEY ARE JUST WEEDS IN A GARDEN.

THEY WILL INEVITABLY SPROUT, BUT DON'T LET THEM TAKE OVER THE GOOD STUFF, LIKE YOUR GRATITUDE, ACCEPTANCE, AND SELF-EMPOWERMENT.

OUR FEARS REVEAL WHAT WE CARE ABOUT THE MOST

WHAT ARE SOME OF YOUR DEEPEST FEARS?

HOW TO make friends WITH FEAR

STEP 1:

WHEN YOU FEEL FEAR ARISE, WELCOME IT AND SIT TOGETHER QUIETLY.

GIVE IT PERMISSION TO TAKE UP SPACE.

reminder:

YOU ARE NOT YOUR THOUGHTS.

STEP 2:

THANK YOUR FEAR FOR JOINING YOU & ASK WHAT IT'S TRYING TO SHOW YOU. IT'S OK IF THE ANSWER DOESN'T COME IMMEDIATELY. FEAR MIGHT BE A LITTLE SHY & CONFUSED AT FIRST.

STEP 3:

ONCE FEAR FEELS SEEN AND HEARD
MAYBE IT WILL
· OPEN · UP · TO · YOU ·

THIS MAY BE THE BEGINNING
OF A BEAUTIFUL FRIENDSHIP.

STEP 4:

NOW THAT YOU ARE IN A RELATIONSHIP
WITH FEAR, ASK POLITELY AND SOFTLY
IF YOU MAY DUST IT OFF TO SEE MORE
CLEARLY WHAT IT HAS TO TEACH YOU.

BRING
COMPASSION
TO WHAT
YOU LEARN.

MAYBE IT'S
HARD TO FIGURE
IT ALL OUT.
THAT IS OK.
YOU ARE OK.

GET TO THE
ROOTS

SELF-ACCEPTANCE IS A PROCESS

WHAT DO YOU LOVE ABOUT YOURSELF?

WAYS TO CULTIVATE SELF-COMPASSION:

WE ARE OFTEN FOCUSED ON WHAT WE WANT TO BECOME. TAKE A MOMENT TO REMEMBER OR LIST SOME THINGS *you already have become.*

IN LITTLE WAYS EVERY DAY, TREAT YOURSELF WITH THE SAME LEVEL OF KINDNESS YOU WOULD TREAT SOMEONE ELSE YOU DEEPLY RESPECT.

IF THERE IS SOMETHING YOU HAVE A HARD TIME ACCEPTING ABOUT YOURSELF ON YOUR OWN, CONFIDE IN SOMEONE CLOSE TO YOU.

REPLACE A BAD HABIT with a good one.

WHEN YOUR NEGATIVE VOICE DISHES OUT SELF-CRITICISM, RESPOND TO IT WITH SELF-APPROVAL AND ACCEPTANCE BY THINKING OF SOMETHING YOU LIKE ABOUT YOURSELF.

CREATE A POSITIVE AFFIRMATION FOR YOURSELF BY OBSERVING A NEGATIVE BELIEF AND WRITING THE OPPOSITE AS A POSITIVE STATEMENT IN THE PRESENT TENSE AS IF IT WERE ALREADY TRUE.

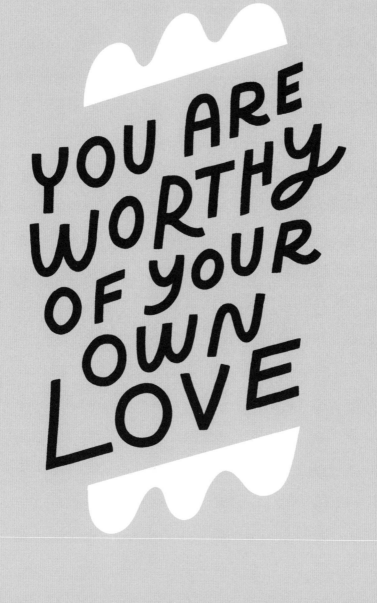

CREATIVITY BRINGS YOU CLOSER TO YOURSELF

WHAT FEELS CREATIVELY FULFILLING TO YOU?

WAYS TO USE CREATIVITY ...TO... EXPLORE YOURSELF:

PLAY

GO WILD WITH ART SUPPLIES, *DANCE FOR FUN*, OR EXPERIMENT WITH MATERIALS IN *UNEXPECTED WAYS* AND SEE WHAT TAKES SHAPE.

express

YOUR THOUGHTS AND EMOTIONS USING words, COLOR, LINE, MOVEMENT, LIGHT, OR SHAPES.

plan

A SIMPLE CREATIVE ACTIVITY
YOU CAN *DEVOTE* YOURSELF TO
·»»»» ON A REGULAR BASIS «««·
AND *LET IT BECOME* YOUR

creative practice.

SUPER IMPORTANT REMINDER: YOU ARE ALLOWED
TO PRIORITIZE YOUR CREATIVE TIME. MAKING ART
IS NOT SELFISH; IT'S SELF-CARE. YOU DESERVE IT!

LEARN A NEW CRAFT TO PUSH YOURSELF BEYOND YOUR ♡COMFORT ZONE♡ AND NOTICE WHAT FEELINGS COME UP.

◉ OBSERVE ◉

REFLECT ON HOW YOUR CREATIVITY HELPS YOU TO
RESPOND TO YOURSELF AND THE WORLD AROUND YOU.
WHAT YOU DISCOVER MAY LEAD YOU TO CLEARER
SELF-UNDERSTANDING AND NEW INSPIRATION.

YOUR UNIQUENESS IS A GIFT

WHEN DO YOU FEEL THE MOST CONNECTED WITH THE REAL YOU?

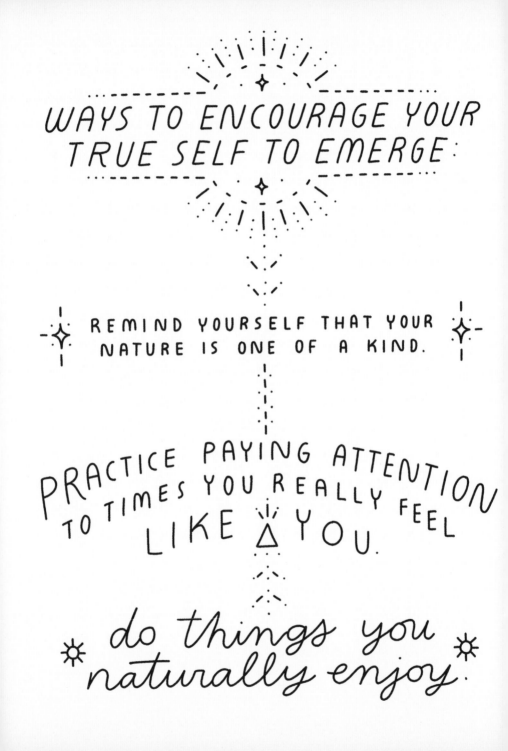

WAYS TO ENCOURAGE YOUR TRUE SELF TO EMERGE:

REMIND YOURSELF THAT YOUR NATURE IS ONE OF A KIND.

PRACTICE PAYING ATTENTION TO TIMES YOU REALLY FEEL LIKE △ YOU.

do things you naturally enjoy.

SPEAK HONESTLY AND OPENLY ABOUT THINGS THAT ARE MEANINGFUL TO YOU.

ACT WITH · INTENTION · AND USE YOUR EVERYDAY ENDEAVORS AS WAYS TO CHANNEL YOURSELF.

REMINDER:
DON'T LET THE IDEA OF PLEASING OTHERS
BLOCK YOU. WHAT OTHER PEOPLE THINK
OF YOU IS BEYOND YOUR CONTROL.
BE AUTHENTIC ANYWAY.

WE
ARE IN A
CONSTANT
STATE OF
GROWTH &
CHANGE

WHAT HELPS YOU TO GROW AND SHIFT?

OPTIMAL CONDITIONS FOR GROWTH

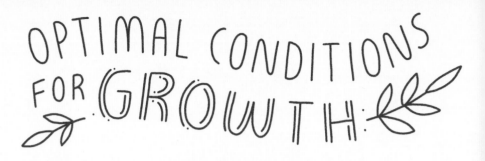

WARM SUNLIGHT

nourishment

CARE

SPACE

TIME

SUPPORT SYSTEMS

PERIODS OF **DARKNESS**

A CONTEMPLATION PRACTICE
FOR EMBRACING CHANGE:

SITUATE YOURSELF IN A COMFORTABLE SEATED POSITION IN A ···CALM··· ENVIRONMENT.

CLOSE YOUR EYES AND BEGIN TO NOTICE THE EVER-PRESENT CURRENT OF ENERGY THAT CHANNELS THROUGH YOU AND ALL LIVING BEINGS.

THINK ABOUT HOW REMARKABLE IT IS THAT THE CELLS IN YOUR BODY ARE IN CONSTANT STATES OF REGENERATION: ON SOME LEVEL YOU ARE NEVER THE EXACT SAME PHYSICAL BEING, MOMENT TO MOMENT.

sit with what you are feeling for as long as you'd like.

LET THIS VIEW OF CHANGE INSPIRE YOU TO BE FLUID AND ADAPTIVE THROUGH ALL OF YOUR SHIFTS, BIG AND SMALL, ♡ WITH OPENNESS AND ACCEPTANCE.♡

ALLOW YOURSELF TO EVOLVE

WHAT DOES TRUSTING THE PROCESS LOOK LIKE TO YOU?

SMALL, EVERYDAY PRACTICES TO CULTIVATE *Patience*

WHEN YOU ARE FEELING
IMPATIENT,
······ REMEMBER ·····
THAT THIS MOMENT IS
JUST AS IMPORTANT
--- AS THE NEXT. ---

ENVISION YOUR JOURNEY AS A SERIES
OF UNIQUE EVENTS STRUNG TOGETHER
LIKE A *garland* OF FLOWERS,
EACH ONE BLOOMING
IN · ITS · OWN · TIME
···ALONG THE WAY.···

CHECK IN WITH YOURSELF REGULARLY TO ASSESS YOUR CURRENT STATE OF BEING.

COLLECT EVIDENCE: LOG MEMORIES WITH PHOTOS OR WRITING TO REFLECT ON WHAT HAS PASSED AND TO KEEP YOURSELF GROUNDED IN THE *Present moment*

✳ REMIND YOURSELF ✳ THAT WHAT'S MEANT TO COME WILL, AND IT WILL BE WORTH THE WAIT.

EVERYTHING
DOESN'T HAVE
TO BE OK ALL
OF THE TIME

HOW CAN YOU GIVE YOURSELF SPACE TO PROCESS NEGATIVE EMOTIONS?

WAYS TO MAKE PEACE  WITH YOUR DARK TIMES:

NOT ALL PARTS OF BEING ALIVE ARE EXCITING, BUT ALL CAN BE HONORED AS PARTS OF THE HUMAN EXPERIENCE.

when you are experiencing — — — sadness: — — —

REMEMBER THAT A NEGATIVE FEELING IS NORMAL AND OK, AND *IT DOESN'T DEFINE YOU.*

GREET IT.

BREATHE WITH IT.

BE ALONE WITH IT IN THE DARK.

TRY *journaling* YOUR STREAM OF CONSCIOUSNESS TO SLOW YOUR MIND DOWN AND 👁 SEE 👁 YOUR THOUGHTS *more clearly.*

TALK ABOUT IT ··· WITH A ··· FELLOW HUMAN.

CHANGE YOUR ENVIRONMENT TO ONE IN WHICH YOU FEEL SUPPORTED.

AS HARD AS IT CAN BE, TRY TO BE THANKFUL FOR THE DARKNESS, FRAMING IT AS AN EXPERIENCE THAT ACTIVATES A SPECIFIC PART OF YOURSELF TO EXPLORE.

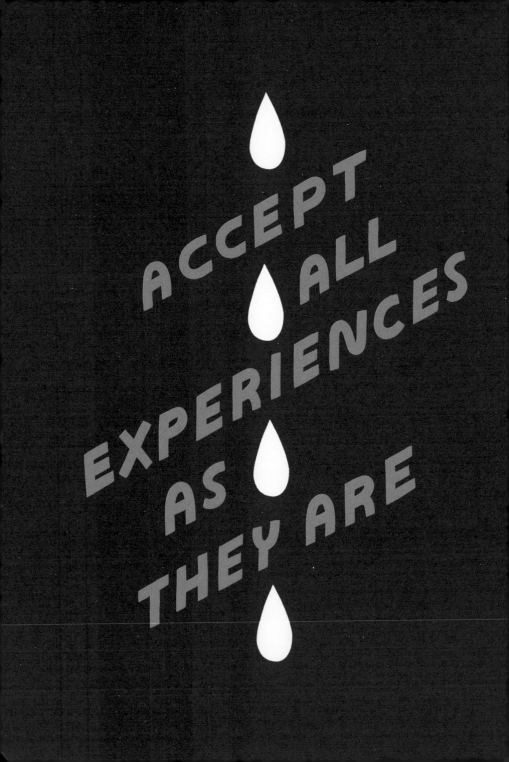

NEW SEEDS NEED SPACE TO OPEN UP

WHAT ARE SOME NEW THINGS YOU'D LIKE TO START?

rituals FOR renewal,

FOR WHEN YOU NEED A NEW BEGINNING:

PRUNE & RE-POT YOUR HOUSEPLANTS.

ORGANIZE & CLEAN A CLUTTERED SPACE.

BURY A FLOWER SEED & WHISPER LOVING WORDS TO IT.

GET A HAIR-CUT!

EXHALE ALL THE WA

CLEAR YOUR MIND BY
SPILLING YOUR THOUGHTS OUT
IN WRITING OR TO A
TRUSTED FRIEND.

DONATE A BOX
OF STUFF YOU
DON'T NEED.

LIE DOWN IN A QUIET SPACE
AND CLOSE YOUR EYES. DECIDE
THAT IN THIS MOMENT YOU
ARE OPEN TO NEWNESS AND
TRUST IT WILL COME YOUR WAY.

Allow yourself to move forward by forgiving yourself for the past.

TIP: DO ANY OF THESE THINGS ON THE
NEW)) :: ((MOON.

ANY MOMENT CAN BE A NEW BEGINNING

THERE IS ALWAYS SOMETHING TO BE THANKFUL FOR

WHAT ARE YOU GRATEFUL FOR?

EVERYDAY PRACTICES TO CULTIVATE
✦ GRATITUDE ✦

TAKE ANY MOMENT TO STOP AND
BE WHERE YOU ARE, AND THANK
THE SPACE AROUND YOU.

 THINK ABOUT
HOW MANY
SIMPLE GIFTS
LIFE GIVES
YOU ON A
DAILY BASIS.

WRITE THANK-YOU NOTES TO PEOPLE
WHO LOVE YOU. THEY WILL FEEL APPRECIATED
AND LOVE THEMSELVES MORE FOR IT, TOO.

WHISPER AN ENTHUSIASTIC
"thank you"
INTO THE OPEN BLUE SKY.

SHARE YOUR GRATEFULNESS BY GIVING
··· BACK AND BEING OF SERVICE. ···

CHERISH NATURE BY THANKING:

A
BUDDING
FLOWER

A
HONEYBEE

THE
WARM
DESERT
SAND

A TALL,
WISE
TREE

THE DIRT
BENEATH YOU

A
GLORIOUS
WATERFALL

A SYNCHRONIZED FLOCK OF BIRDS

AN EXCEPTIONALLY GOLDEN SUNRISE

IT'S OK TO
NOT FULLY
UNDERSTAND

WHAT ARE WAYS YOU CAN BE COMFORTABLE WITH THE UNKNOWN?

A GUIDE TO SURRENDERING TO MYSTERY

 STEP 1:

ON A DARK CLEAR NIGHT, VENTURE OUT TO A PLACE WHERE YOU CAN SEE THE SKY.

STEP 2:

LAY YOUR BODY FACE UP ON THE EARTH AND FEEL YOUR PERSPECTIVE BEGIN TO SHIFT.

⚠ WARNING: SUDDEN FEELINGS OF AWE, SMALLNESS, AND CURIOSITY MAY SPONTANEOUSLY OCCUR.

STEP 3:
REMIND YOURSELF THAT THERE ARE SO MANY UNKNOWNS, AND LET THAT HUMBLE YOU.